ReMind™

Building Rocks *of* Mindfulness

with *Jewish* Stepping Stones

Mara M. Zimmerman

Balboa Press books may be ordered through booksellers or by contacting:

Balboa Press
A Division of Hay House
1663 Liberty Drive
Bloomington, IN 47403
www.balboapress.com
844-682-1282

Because of the dynamic nature of the Internet, any web addresses or links contained in this book may have changed since publication and may no longer be valid. The views expressed in this work are solely those of the author and do not necessarily reflect the views of the publisher, and the publisher hereby disclaims any responsibility for them.

Any people depicted in stock imagery provided by Getty Images are models, and such images are being used for illustrative purposes only.
Certain stock imagery © Getty Images.

Interior Image Credit: Mara M. Zimmerman

ISBN: 979-8-7652-3815-8 (sc)
ISBN: 979-8-7652-3817-2 (e)

Library of Congress Control Number: 2023900968

Print information available on the last page.

Balboa Press rev. date: 05/16/2023

A guided meditation

Shalom

שָׁלוֹם

Imagine
peace.

Inner peace,
world peace,
peace of mind.

Shema

שְׁמַע

Hear, listen.

Good posture,
balanced breathing.

Kavod

כָּבוֹד

Respect yourself,
respect others.

Ahavah

אַהֲבָה

Love yourself,
love others.

Tikkun Olam

תִּיקוּן עוֹלָם

Repair yourself,
repair the world.

Tefillah

תְּפִילָה

Prayer,
service of the heart.

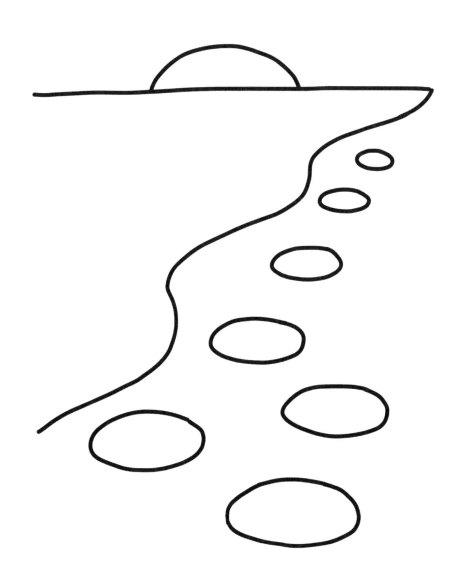

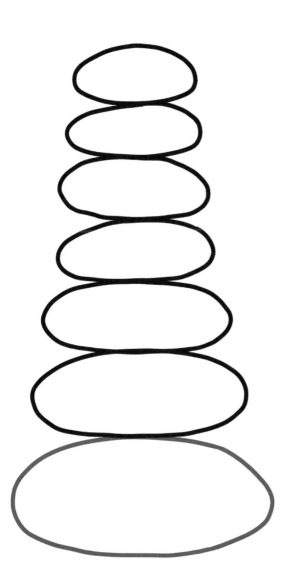

Kavanah

כַּוָּנָה

Intention,
good intentions

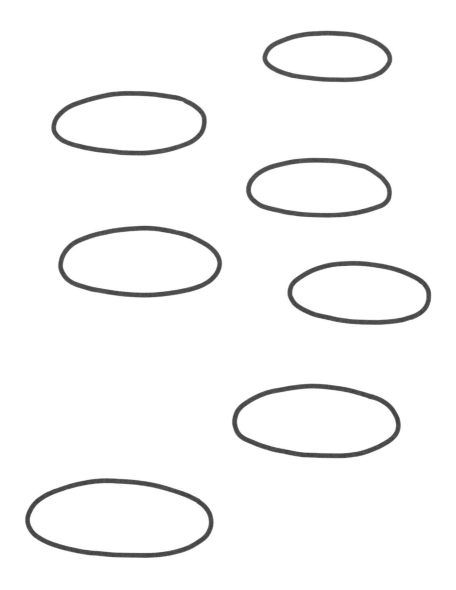

Be present, pay attention, believe in yourself.

Breathe

Ruach

רוּחַ

Spirit of
life

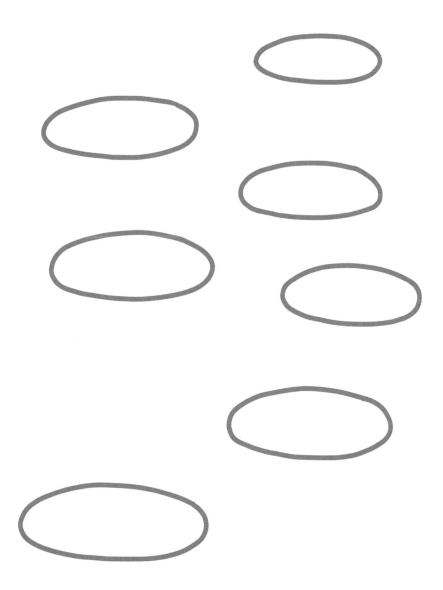

Laugh, play, dance, smile.

Breathe

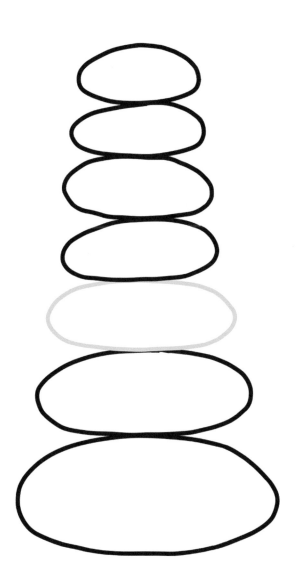

Menuchah

מְנוּחָה

Rest,
relax,
recharge

Pause, energize, balance, movement, stillness.

Breathe

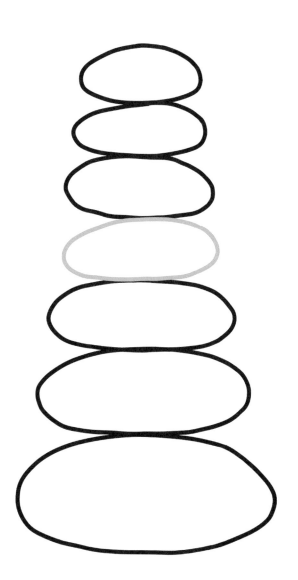

Chesed

חֶסֶד

Loving-kindness,
compassion

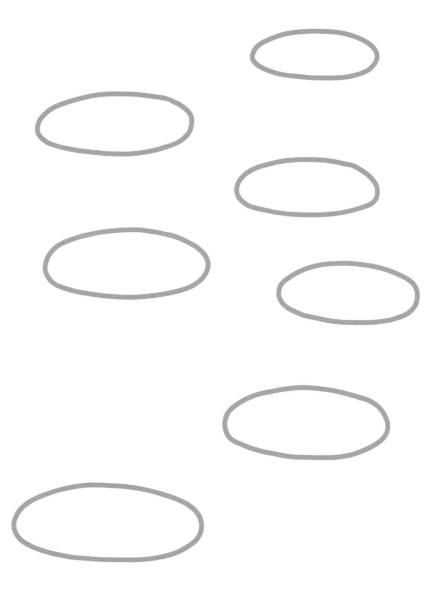

Heart centered, self-care, courage, creativity, gratitude.

Breathe

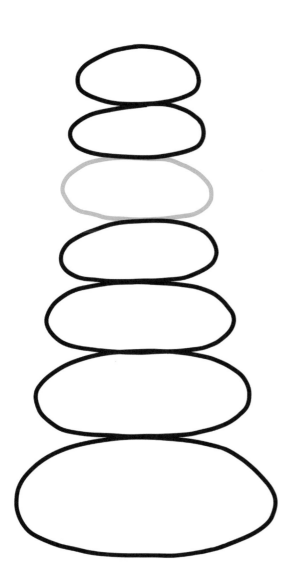

Nefesh

נֶפֶשׁ

Soul,
self,
essence

Community, communication, thoughts,
feelings, nature, inner nature.

Breathe

Hashkatah

הַשְׁקָטָה

Quieting
the
mind,
calm

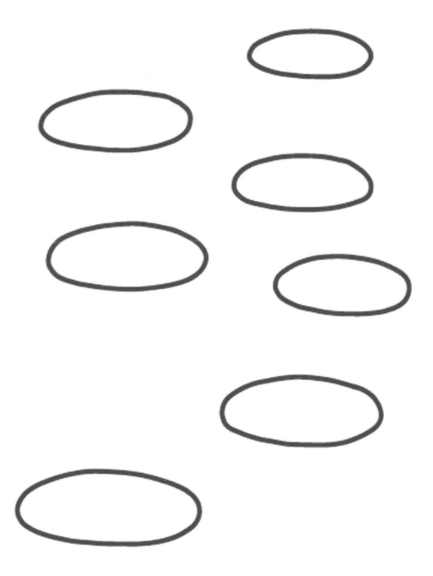

Blessings, tradition, song, chant, sound, silence.

Breathe

Neshamah

נְשָׁמָה

Spiritual,
soulful,
awareness

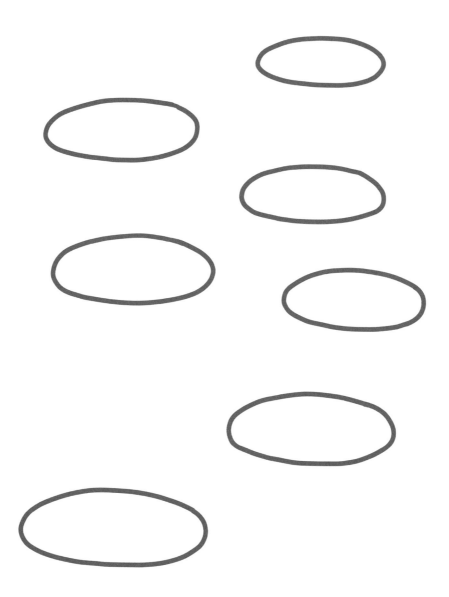

Higher Power, Higher Self, True Self, Best Self.

Breathe

Hatchalah

הַתחָלָה

Beginning

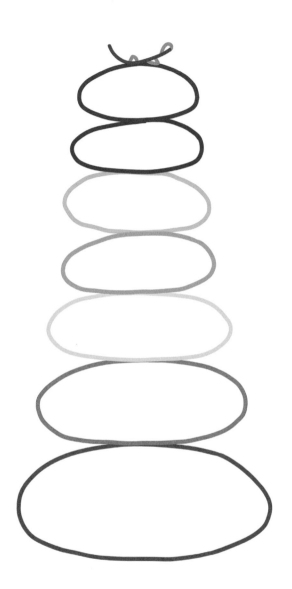

Hatchalah Chadashah

הַתְחָלָה חָדָשׁה

New beginning

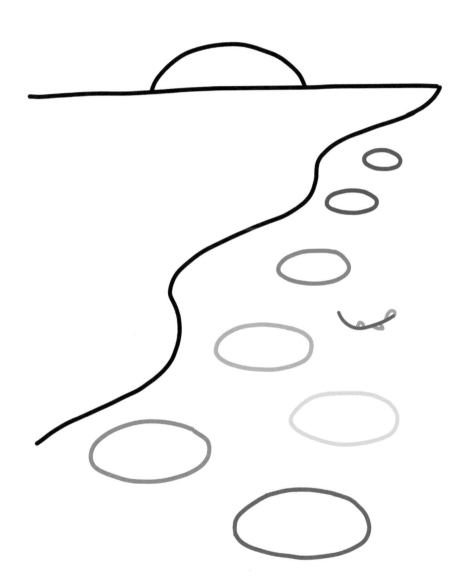

Life חַי Chai

Shalom

שָׁלוֹם

ReMind

About the Author

Mara M. Zimmerman has been teaching meditation and mindfulness in educational and therapeutic spaces throughout her career. She is the author of *Remind:Building Rocks of Mindfulness with Stepping Stones* and *How to Meditate and Why*.

For more information, please visit
maramzimmerman.com

Printed in the United States
by Baker & Taylor Publisher Services